Hand Drawn For my kids

D d

dog

D D D

O O O

G G G

E e

Elephant

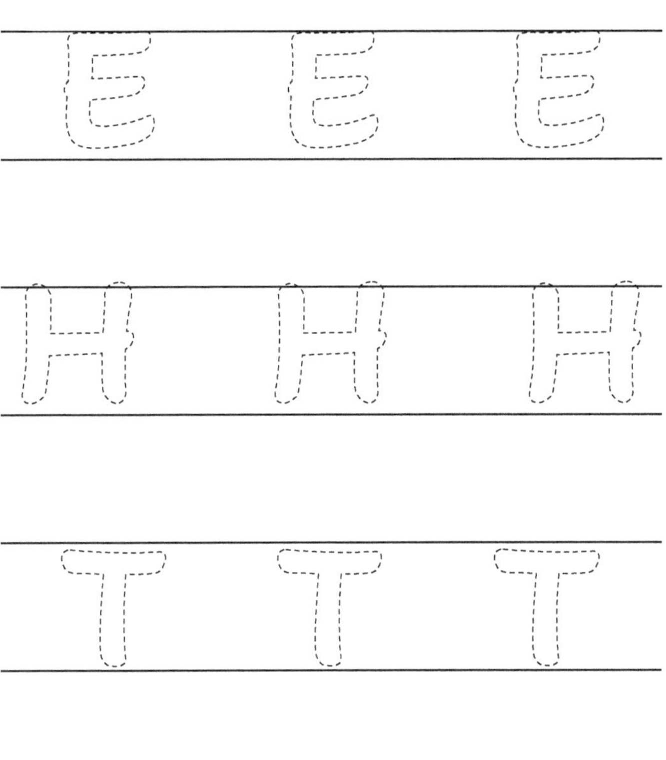

R r

Rabbit

R R R

B B B

T T T

C c

CAT

C C C

A A A

C C C

H h

hyena

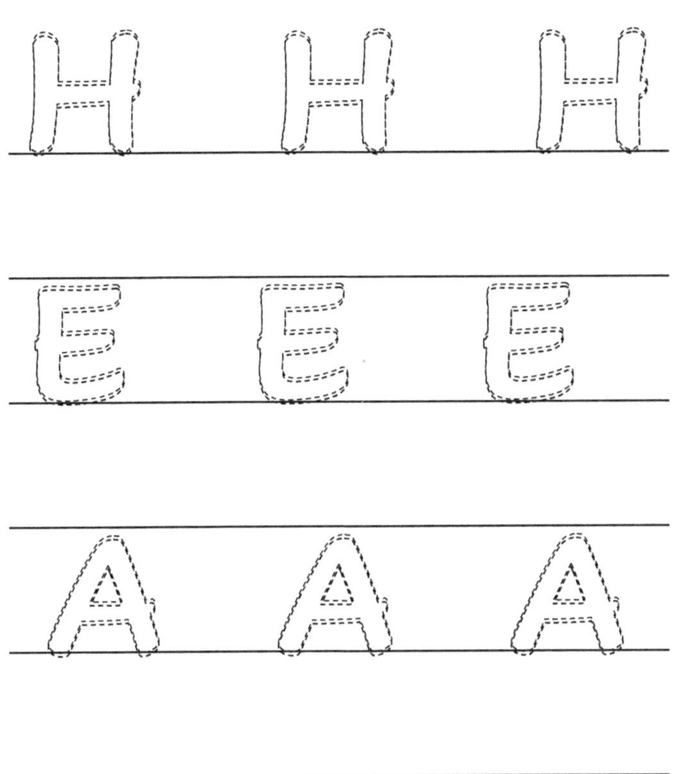

A a

Pig

p p p

i i i

g g g

E e

Eagle

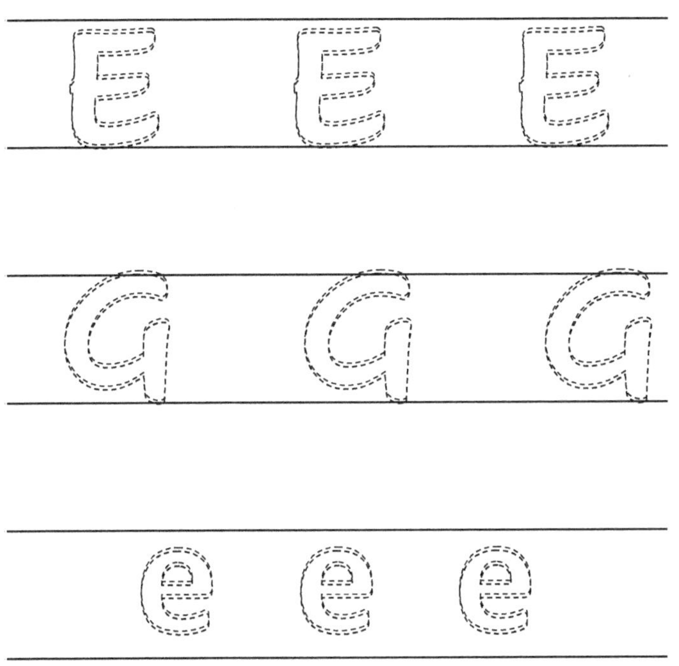

Its color

F f

Fish

F F F

s s s

h h h

M m

The mouse

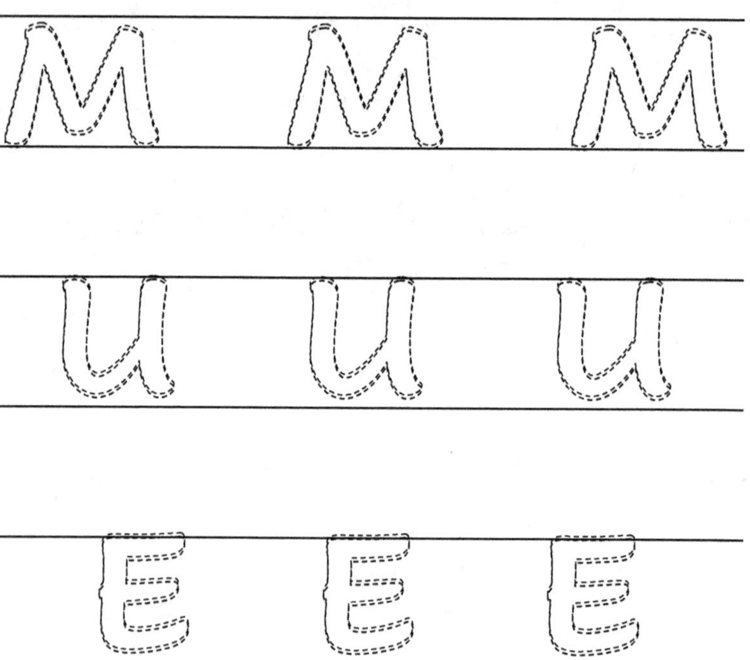

B b

The bird

B B B

R R R

D D D

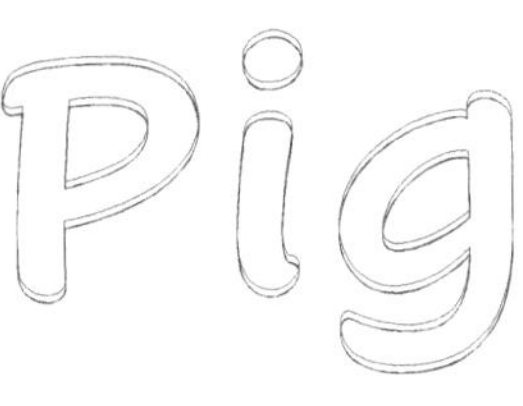

DOG

Hello, My name is Younes and I am from Morocco. If I read this text one day, I will tell you that you are a smart kid and thank you for using my book to develop your abilities in science and knowledge.

Thank you, mom and dad, for caring for your children and providing them with everything for a happy life.